WHEN STRAIGHT
Lines Aren't

JACINTA HUDSON

Copyright © September 2021 Jacinta Hudson

All rights reserved. No part of this book may be reproduced without the written consent of the copyright holder except in the case of quotations for a book review.

Cover Design by Stone Ridge Books

ISBN: 978-0-6489289-4-2

To Brad

The reason I am able to do what I love.
Every book I write is dedicated to you.
Thank you
x

❧

Baby, it's a new day.
So, have a drink on me.
It's time to bring in a new year.

Baby, it's a new month.
Let's wipe the slate clean.
Raise your glass and let's cheer.

Baby, it's a new week.
And I'm feeling free.
Someone bring more wine here.

Because baby, it's a new year,
And we all need to be.
Saying goodbye to last year.

❧

The silence in the noise.
The happiness in tears.
The different things they mean.
Throughout the many years.

❧

This step that I'm taking, it scares me.
And I'm not really sure how it'll end.
All I know is I can't keep going on this way.
And I'm tired of having to pretend.

WHEN STRAIGHT LINES AREN'T

৯৮

Late night notes in my little notebook.
Just trying to stay awake while you cry.
Late night notes in my little notebook.
You laugh at my yawn. I'm so tired I want to die.

৯৮

Close your eyes and dream of a land,
Where nothing is wrong, and everything is fine.
Close your eyes as I hold your hand.
And everything will be alright.

❦

I watch you sleep.
Bum high in the air.
And all my troubles melt away.
I watch you sleep.
Not a care anywhere.
You make all my worries drift away.

❦

Little burrito baby.
My heart is wrapped up in you.
Little burrito baby.
You made all my dreams come true.

WHEN STRAIGHT LINES AREN'T

❦

I'll never get over loving you.
It's something that I'll always do.
No matter just how big or small.
You'll always be my baby.

I'll never stop protecting you.
Hail or shine, I'll push on through.
This will never change.
You'll always be my baby.

I'll never give up embracing you.
In every way you are, I'll encourage your inner truth.
Small or grown I'll nurture you.
You'll always be my baby.

JACINTA HUDSON

I feel for you sweetheart, I really do.
No one in the world feels the way you do.
The thought of your pain, it makes me shudder.
But just for a moment, think about it from us others.

You have never been alone, despite you pushing us away.
You've never been the only one to feel that kind of pain.
And even though we're different,
That doesn't mean that we can't share.
Comparing others to your own life will never turn out fair.

Embrace your whole community, the lucky and the lone.
You'll find love within that unity and, in people, you'll find home.

WHEN STRAIGHT LINES AREN'T

Can you hear my voice,
Screaming across the din?
Can you hear the pain I feel,
Held deep down within?

Can you hear my fear?
Can you see it on my face?
Can you feel my footsteps,
As I quicken up my pace?

Can you feel my heart,
As it beats within my chest?
Can you understand,
How there's never any rest?

Do you see my life,
From underneath your shoe?
Can you see through my eyes,
Or is your sight reserved for you?

Let's all count our blessings.
Let us all pause for a time.
Let's all forgive our misgivings.
And think on what turned out just fine.

Let's all see the silver shining.
From around all those gloomy old clouds.
Let's smile upon that pretty lining.
And of our strength, let us be proud.

Let us embrace each other dearly.
And piece together our holes.
A rough year has cut us so clearly.
But together we can make ourselves whole.

WHEN STRAIGHT LINES AREN'T

Muster up your courage.
Ignite your fire within.
Light the fuse to your firework.
And let your show begin.

Decide your rules at the beginning.
Or wing it from start to end.
But take every step your own way.
Keep your will strong; don't let it bend.

JACINTA HUDSON

❧

Hide away that sniffle.
Don't let them see.
Cover up that cough.
Don't let them hear that sneeze.

What a strange world.
This has come to be.
People have become so fearful.
Of anything less than perfectly healthy.

WHEN STRAIGHT LINES AREN'T

❧

Why am I even here?
Why do I even try?
Just trying to put myself out there.
Then I'm left wondering why.

Why do I even bother?
It's not like you're hearing me speak.
I'm trying to rise and raise my voice.
Instead, I'm left feeling weak.

JACINTA HUDSON

❧

The curser blinks at me.
Blink blink blink.
Why is it so hard to,
Think think think?
Just finish this sentence and it will be,
Done done done.
All I need is a sentence.
Just one one one.
I've been writing this book for so,
Long long long.
It plays over my mind like a,
Song song song.
So why can't I finish this,
Page page page.
It feels like it's taking an,
Age age age.
Once it's complete I'll have,
Won won won.
I just need one more line.
Like this one one one.
How can something you love bring so much,
Pain pain pain?
To finish this book will drive me,
Insane insane insane.

WHEN STRAIGHT LINES AREN'T

༄༅

1, 2, 3, 4
Don't forget to lock the door.
2, 3, 4, 5
Keep the indoor plants alive.
3, 4, 5, 6
Add some veggies to the list.
4, 5, 6, 7
Be in bed before 11.
5, 6, 7, 8
Pay the bills before they're late.
6, 7, 8, 9
Get the kids to school on time.
7, 8, 9, 10
Scrap the list and start again.
1, 2, 3, 4
Run some errands, head to the store.
2, 3, 4, 5
Teach your eldest how to drive.
3, 4, 5, 6
It's my endless to-do list.
4, 5, 6, 7…

JACINTA HUDSON

Baby girl,
You were so little when we met.
And now you're oh so tall.
Little man,
With such chubby little cheeks.
Watching you grow has been a ball.
Cutie pies,
You came into our lives,
With such a chaotic whirl.
Pumpkin pie,
How I would die,
To protect you, my little girl.
Handsome man,
We waited so long,
To see your beautiful face.
And one yet to come,
Come sooner please.
We're excited to be touched by your grace.
So many hearts,
With so much love to give.
And a whole wide world to explore.
And with all of my heart,
I will live,
To ensure you get what you want and much more.

Family first.
I'll always be,
Standing by your side.

Family first.
I'm next to you,
With my head held high.

Family first.
I'll hold your hand,
Through low and higher tides.

Family first.
I'll call you mine,
And I'll do so filled with pride.

JACINTA HUDSON

I'm looking forward to Christmas.
More so this year than before.
I'm looking forward to embracing you,
The moment you walk through the door.

I'm looking forward to Christmas.
I'm excited for the gifts and the food.
I'm looking forward to carols.
And the overall joyous mood.

WHEN STRAIGHT LINES AREN'T

❧

I'm decorating early this year.
I don't really care what you say.
The decos came out of the box today.
Because I'm decorating early this year.

I'm wrapping early this year.
The presents are there.
So, I don't really care.
I'm wrapping early this year.

I'm playing music early this year.
The merry old tunes,
Will put me in the mood.
So, I'm playing music early this year.

I'm spreading joy early this year.
We all need some cheer,
To send off a hard year.
So, I'm spreading joy early this year.

JACINTA HUDSON

They say that you've had fun.
You're the excited happy one.
That your days are always full of love and laughter.
But your face tells another story.
It's so void of any glory.
And it's just a simple smile that I am after.

WHEN STRAIGHT LINES AREN'T

Quality vs quantity.
A constant source of pain.
One that art demands we give our attention.
Because a lack of focus.
Results in a lack of gain.
And a war between the two creates some tension.

JACINTA HUDSON

❧

The sun on your face.
The sweet gentle breeze.
The way that the season can put you at ease.
The smiles and the laughter.
The way the kids play.
Summer can literally melt your troubles away.

❧

Hold a place for this moment in time.
Don't let it slip away.
Soon it will vanish from all but your mind.
But in your heart, it will stay.

WHEN STRAIGHT LINES AREN'T

☙❧

Change is in the air.
Change is everywhere.
It creeps up on you when you're not watching,
And ruffles up your hair.

Keep your eyes wide open.
And take life by the balls.
And when the changes overwhelm you,
Try to embrace them all.

JACINTA HUDSON

Wash it, brush it, style it.
Do it this way please.
If you want some volume,
You need to give it a tease.
Part it over here now,
And flip it over there.
When did it get so complicated?
Did we forget it's only hair?

Brush and blend and sprinkle,
Some powder on your cheeks.
I still can't get it right.
Though I've been practicing for weeks.
Shave it, wax it, tan it.
See all the followers I've got.
For every new like I gain,
I have to wonder what I've lost.

WHEN STRAIGHT LINES AREN'T

Procrastination is the devil.
She's disguised as pretty things.
They're oh so sweet and entertaining.
But not a scrap of wealth they bring.

If you listen very closely,
You can hear your passions fade.
You can watch your vision bloom and grow.
Or procrastinate your days away.

JACINTA HUDSON

Hush my darling.
Mummy's here.
I'll hold you close and warm.

Hush my darling.
Don't you fear.
I'll protect you from the storm.

Hush my darling.
Don't you cry.
I'll stay right by your side.

Hush my darling.
Close your eyes.
And sleep throughout the night.

WHEN STRAIGHT LINES AREN'T

☙❧

Your face lights up and it warms my heart.
I'm so pleased to see you happy.
You've been spoiled today and it's just a little part,
Of what I'll do to make you happy.

☙❧

Brilliantly bright, your light blinds me.
A marvellous thing from the start.
Beautifully bound, your love binds me.
You'll always have a piece of my heart.

JACINTA HUDSON

❦

There's a certain type of ache that you don't know.
It's the kind that those who suffer from will rarely ever show.
Because they have their little bundle in their arms.
So, who would ever think that all that joy could have come from any harm?

There's a certain kind of pain that comes from birth.
When your plans don't go your way and you're questioning your worth.
While everyone is happy baby's here.
But all you want to do is hide away and disappear.

There's a certain kind of grief that comes from loss.
When those around you take control while you want to call the shots.
It's not that you haven't come to love the view.
But it wasn't the path that you had planned to pursue.

There's a certain type of emotion that you feel.
When you have to come to terms with fantasy being different from what is real.
It's a frustrating, saddening, crippling need to scream.
One that no one else can feel, because they didn't share your dream.

WHEN STRAIGHT LINES AREN'T

❧

I pray for you.
Because there just isn't another word.
I pray for you.
To describe the state of the world.
I pray for you.
And I hope you can hear me now.
I pray for you.
Because I don't know another way how.
I pray for you.
To describe the way that I feel.
I pray for you.
I see that your pain is real.
I pray for you.
And I hope one day we can heal.
I pray for you.
But right now, it all seems surreal.
I pray for you.
It is time to move past this war.
I pray for you.
Moving through a better door.
I pray for you.
Until then I will fall to my knees.
I pray for you.
And beg for a better world please.
As I pray for you.

JACINTA HUDSON

❧

I know you see me.
The way that I see you.
I know that you get me.
Because I get you too.
And I thank you for being there.
When I needed you.
So, here's to another year.
That we both got through.

WHEN STRAIGHT LINES AREN'T

❦

Just 10 minutes.
That's all you need.
To start a new task on your list.
Just 10 little minutes.
To get out of your head.
And tackle just one little bit.
That 10 small minutes.
Can grow in a blink.
And suddenly you've done so much more.
Start with 10 little minutes.
And then you've made a small start.
And that is more than before.

JACINTA HUDSON

Mummy I adore you,
From my place in the sky.
Mummy I miss you,
As I fly up high.
Mummy I love you,
And we'll never know why,
I had to leave you.
Just know that I'm fine.

WHEN STRAIGHT LINES AREN'T

These scratches are fresh, and they hurt me.
They burn when you touch them so roughly.
I need you to handle me gently.
As I take a little time to heal.

These scars are still fresh and they're painful.
The way that you poke them is hurtful.
I'm trying, but I feel so unstable.
As I take a little more time to heal.

JACINTA HUDSON

I don't know if you know this,
But you intimidate me.
I find you overwhelming.
You seem to have it all worked out.
I don't know if you know this.
In you, an angel I do see.
You radiate brilliance.
So smart and sweet and beautiful.
I don't know if you know this,
But I wish that we could be,
Closer than we are now.
I would love to know you better.
I don't know if you know this,
But you make me believe,
That I can be much better.
If I just work a little harder.

WHEN STRAIGHT LINES AREN'T

❦

The gratitude I feel cannot be measured out.
This is something very real that I am feeling.
I've been showered with so much love.
And now my head is reeling.

My heart is full and happy.
I feel the sun on me shining.
Surrounded by family who embrace me so.
All around me is gold and silver lining.

JACINTA HUDSON

Christmas baby.
It's the best time of the year.
An entire season,
Where people embrace cheer.
Christmas baby.
As beautiful as a dove.
When all the lights fill the streets.
And our hearts are filled with love.

WHEN STRAIGHT LINES AREN'T

❦

This year sucks, it's time for a new one.
Let's say goodbye to 2020.
This year's been rough, let's move on to a new one.
Let's say goodbye to the pain.
From fires to finances, the weight has been heavy.
Let's bring on 2021.
From destruction to death, we've all had enough.
Let's never do that again.

JACINTA HUDSON

I'm the outcast, the pariah, the disappointment, and the shame.
I'm the one who took your son away from glory, wealth, and fame.
I'm the shock, the stab, the gut wrench to all that you held dear.
I'm the devil in high heels, your worst nightmare, your worst fear.
I might be very different from the girl you did expect.
But I'm also something important, so listen closely pet.
I'm the one that he has chosen, and I've no plans to go away.
Because we love each other dearly, so it's by his side I'll stay.

WHEN STRAIGHT LINES AREN'T

Can you try and see me, for who I really am?
If I'm always expected to measure up, know that I never can.
Just because I'm different doesn't mean I'm not enough.
I'm doing my best to fit in here, being the outcast can be rough.
Even though it can be difficult, I'm determined to push through.
I don't have to meet the standards to get closer to you.
I will show you my true colours, you will see me shining bright.
You will fall in love with my true self. I will show you I am right.

JACINTA HUDSON

☙❧

Let's start a competition.
Of who can read the most.
Pick up a book.
Let's take a look.
And have a little boast.

It'll be a little fun.
To take us through the year.
Then at the end,
When I beat you, my friend,
You'll hear me howl and cheer.

WHEN STRAIGHT LINES AREN'T

❧

There's an alien in my belly and it's trying to get out.
It claws at every angle, no matter how often I shout.
It doesn't know it hurts me. It's just trying to make some room.
But the truth is I'll forgive it, once it's born, you know I'll swoon.

❧

My head is filled with clubhouse moments.
And wiggly, giggly songs.
But while I pretend they're annoying me.
I'm secretly singing along.

JACINTA HUDSON

When the good is bad.
And the bad is good.
And you don't know how to feel.
How do you know,
Which emotions to show,
And which are the ones to steal?

WHEN STRAIGHT LINES AREN'T

I'll tell you a secret,
I'm not sure that I can do this.
But I'm holding my head up as I try.
I'm fairly sure I'm going to fall.
And I won't quite manage it all.
But that won't stop me from aiming high.

JACINTA HUDSON

Hush child, don't you see,
I'm doing all I can.
Hush child, don't you know,
You changed all of my plans.
Hush child, can't you hear,
I need a chance to rest.
Hush child, calm yourself.
I'm doing my very best.

WHEN STRAIGHT LINES AREN'T

☙❧

Sleep, baby, sleep.
I wish you weren't awake.
Sleep, baby, sleep.
Because mamma needs a break.
Sleep, baby, sleep.
When you wake up, we can play.
But first, sleep, baby, sleep.
Or we won't make it through the day.

JACINTA HUDSON

※

I'm so glad I found you.
Even though I knew you were there.
You were hiding behind life.
And I couldn't work out where.
But you looked around a corner,
And then you called out my name.
And now I'm so grateful you found me.
Because we think so much the same.

WHEN STRAIGHT LINES AREN'T

༄༅

A whole week later and I can't stop smiling.
Remembering the fun that we had.
It's been such a long time since I couldn't stop laughing.
You broke me and I'm oh so glad.
I don't know where you were when I needed you then.
But I get a feeling you're better for me now.
And I feel like we're going to be lifelong friends.
And I can't wait to see it pan out.

JACINTA HUDSON

❧

Being a grown up is hard.
There are too many things to do.
And just when you think you've washed your hands,
There's even more mess thrown at you.

❧

One and two and three and four.
Take one step and then one more.
One and two and three and four.
Soon you'll be walking out the door.

WHEN STRAIGHT LINES AREN'T

Hold your hand out to another,
And help them off the floor.
As it's time to make amends,
For the pain that came before.

It's important to help one another,
To embrace them as a friend.
Otherwise, we'll spend our lives,
Fighting until the end.

JACINTA HUDSON

❦

I am not this person.
This isn't where I thrive.
This is the place where most of my worst fears all come alive.

I am not that human.
This isn't my strong suit.
This is the time someone usually decides that I should get the boot.

This is not my passion.
I need help to see this through.
I feel so alone, but I can't do it on my own.
I need a hand from you.

WHEN STRAIGHT LINES AREN'T

❦

I don't want to write.
Edits will have to wait.
Anxiety is my hook.
And you know I've taken the bait.

I'm trying to find motivation.
I've looked everywhere for my muse.
But the truth is that I'm struggling.
It takes a lot just to put on my shoes.

The weight on my chest is crushing.
The heaviness is weighing me down.
I so want to rise, and to claim my prize.
But really, I'm just trying not to drown.

They say that hindsight is 20-20.
And oh, my how true that has been.
The ups and the downs.
Feeling like you will drown.
Then you look back on where you have been.

WHEN STRAIGHT LINES AREN'T

Deadlines loom and there's work to be done.
I can't put it off any longer.
The lists only grow, and I'm the only one,
Who can tackle the tasks left to do.

I must be smart, and I need to commit.
Laziness will not suffice.
I have to push on and I mustn't quit.
It's time to get on the move.

JACINTA HUDSON

I will stand for what I want.
I will take what I need.
For I deserve more than this chaos.
I will take what I want.
And demand to be freed.
Because my dreams demand more than this chaos.

WHEN STRAIGHT LINES AREN'T

◈◈

It's getting kind of hot in here.
I'm getting all fired up.
Because you don't think that I can win.

But there's an ace up my sleeve.
I've got faith and I believe.
And I'm determined that I will make it all fit in.

Big decisions.
Life revisions.
Changing everything.
Move over world.
Here comes a girl.
Who's conquering everything.

WHEN STRAIGHT LINES AREN'T

Are you ready for my come back?
Are you ready for me now?
Are you ready for me to stand up?
My time to shine is now.

I don't want to eat and tea tastes funny.
I haven't had much sleep today.
There's something weighing heavily on my mind.
But I haven't the courage to say.

I'm terrified of what might happen.
If this is the path we are on.
I'm trying to pretend it's nothing.
But I'm scared I might be wrong.

WHEN STRAIGHT LINES AREN'T

Heart don't fail me now.
Help me get my point across.
Let me find the right descriptions.
To illustrate my loss.

Even though I have so much.
There is still this little hole.
There's a little piece that's missing.
Keeping me from being whole.

I know that I am lucky.
And I know I have a lot.
But I can't help focusing.
On the things that I have not.

JACINTA HUDSON

Little boy blue come blow on your horn,
And let the world know you're here.

I've something important I need you to know,
So, come now and lend me an ear.

Though times are strange, in time all will change,
But one thing will always be clear.

From their voice to their touch,
Mum and dad love you so much,
And in their arms, you'll have nothing to fear.

WHEN STRAIGHT LINES AREN'T

୶୶

Just before you go,
Tell me everything you know.
Tell me all about your life.
Share with me, your best advice.

Before your soul is free,
Promise me you'll never leave.
Swear we'll never be apart.
That you'll stay within my heart.

Just before you go.
There's something you should know.
I'll never lose my faith,
That I'll see you again one day.

JACINTA HUDSON

We live our lives on paper.
From birth until our deaths.
There's a form for every stage we reach.
From education to illustration.
Advice from psyc to dietitian.
Even down to the religions that we preach.

All our lessons are written down.
For others to learn with thoughtful frowns.
As we make our way through the years.
There's no getting off the grid.
It's just the life that we live.
As we document all our hopes and our fears.

We just want to be heard,
Remembered and loved.
So, we tell ourselves there is a way,
To live in the moment,
As we fill in more forms,
To prove that we were there that day.

WHEN STRAIGHT LINES AREN'T

This is my letter to you.
You with your head in your hands.
To remind you to keep on fighting.
When you fall, I'll help you stand.

This is my call out to you.
You with your heart in your gut.
Even when you feel all alone.
I'm here to help you out of that rut.

This is my whisper to you.
You with the noise in your brain.
It's so loud that even I hear it.
And trust me, I feel your pain.

This is my moment for you.
The time when I hold some space.
For the struggles you feel.
And the pain that is real.
It's here that I'll hold you this place.

JACINTA HUDSON

❧

I want to scream without making a sound.
I want to call out for help from loved ones,
But there's no one I can talk to around.
At least no one who will understand.
Or at least there's nothing new to tell them,
So, there's no new way for them to lend a hand.
Just an ear to listen, or maybe a shoulder to cry on.
But it's the generic words of comfort I've come to rely on.
The kind I have to agree with, even though they don't help me.
They just give me things to think about,
For my anxiety to use to hurt me.
Just focus on the positives, they tell me once again.
But they can't feel the heaviness within me.
It's been an open wound for years now, and the agony won't end.
It makes me want to give up on everything I love.
And although I'll never step off that ledge,
I secretly pray to feel a shove.
I don't know how much longer I can go along this way.
But for now, I'll walk along the line,
Between the numbness and the pain.
And just hope that by the grace of god, I'll make it through today.

WHEN STRAIGHT LINES AREN'T

❧

If you can see what I can't see,
Then why not open my eyes?
If you can hear what I can't hear,
Lend me your ear and some peace of mind.
If you can tell that I'm struggling,
Then why won't you draw the line?
Take a moment to connect those dots.
Give me the gift of your time.

If you're aware of what I am not,
Why on earth won't you tell me?
If it's so clear for you to see,
Why can't you just show me?
When my mind's a mess, I cannot express,
How important it is just to show me.
I can't see through the fog. I don't know that I'm bogged.
That's the moment I need you to know me.

Better than I know myself.
They're the moments that I need some help.
For I turn to you,
Because I don't know what to do.
I need answers from somebody else.

You're my strength when I've no other.
You're my best friend and my lover.
You're my legs when I can't stand.
You're my soul mate and my man.
You're the breath I couldn't catch.
You're my polar and my match.
You're everything I'll ever need.
You hold me close and set me free.

WHEN STRAIGHT LINES AREN'T

This is my poem for you.
Because you always know what to do.
This is my chance to say,
That without you I wouldn't be here today.
Here in this place where I'm loved.
Here in this place where I can love.
Right down to my soul.
I know you're the reason that I am whole.
So, this is my inner truth.
A poem to say I love you.

JACINTA HUDSON

You come and you go.
And I never know,
When I'm likely to see your face.

Just when I feel,
Like I've got you for real,
You disappear without a trace.

It's all so real,
The frustration I feel,
As you come and go from this place.

With a blink of an eye,
And without a goodbye,
Sliding up a sleeve like an ace.

WHEN STRAIGHT LINES AREN'T

❧

This is my spot, my spot on the couch.
Don't ask me to move or I'll bite you.
This is my spot, right here on the couch.
Don't tell me to leave or I'll fight you.

❧

It's been a rough year for many.
And I really feel for you all.
I hope that you know if you're struggling.
I'm ready to take your call.

JACINTA HUDSON

꙳

Piles of books surround me.
It's a crazy cluttered mess.
One that will take some time to sort out.
But it appears to be growing.
And the growth doesn't seem to be slowing.
And the challenge of cleaning it up is wearing me out.

WHEN STRAIGHT LINES AREN'T

༄༅

The laughter fades as the anxiety waves.
The light is shrouded in dark.
Tears start to well as anxiety swells.
And gone is the fun at the park.
My world comes to a stop and my heart starts to drop.
I feel myself starting to fall.
I brace for the heat; my heart quickens its beat.
As I hear the anxiety call.

JACINTA HUDSON

❧

Of all the gifts you'll receive for this bub.
The best one's from you, it's the gift of true love.
For there'll never be another throughout this whole world.
Who will love quite as fiercely for your little girl.

❧

I dream about the day that you are family.
When you walk into my house like you live there.
I dream about a time that we coexist happily.
And in all our highs and lows we gladly share.

WHEN STRAIGHT LINES AREN'T

☙❧

I can't contain my excitement.
I can barely control all my joy.
I can't wait to meet your lil princess.
Or your boisterous little boy.

I'm so overjoyed by your announcement.
My heart is so full from your news.
I can't stop my heart from pounding.
I'm beyond happy for the both of you.

JACINTA HUDSON

I'll try not to be offended.
Even as you make me weep.
It's not as though you'd know.
That you would cut me deep.

How could you have seen me?
I only reached out to you.
You only wanted someone else.
What else were you to do?

WHEN STRAIGHT LINES AREN'T

೭୬୯ଚ

It breaks my heart to watch you cry.
I wish I could heal your pain.
It breaks my heart to see you struggle.
I wish I could remove this stain.

Scars remain long after the cut.
But the pain doesn't go away.
Memories go hazy but the feelings remain.
Just pray that they ease one day.

The opposite is attractive.
The same will compliment me.
It's so nice to have a friend like you.
One that can really "get" me.

It's not a big deal to me.
But it might just be for you.
It's just a simple gesture,
But it's something I can do.

WHEN STRAIGHT LINES AREN'T

Such a strange encounter.
An odd way for us to start.
Who knew that many years later,
You'd have a big chunk of my heart?
I've cried upon your shoulder.
You've watched me fall down to my knees.
I'm so blessed you've stuck around,
To see me rise up to my feet.

JACINTA HUDSON

❧❦

My son screamed from his bedroom.
He called out for my help.
He told me "Mum, I want food."
But all I had was kelp.
I gave him a bottle to drink up.
But he would have none of it.
So, I put the bottle back in the kitchen.
And he went back to his fit.

WHEN STRAIGHT LINES AREN'T

Take a breath. 1, 2, 3.
Count along with me.

Let it out. 1, 2, 3.
It's easy you will see.

When you're stressed. 1, 2, 3.
Before you start to flee.

Take a breath. 1, 2, 3.
Let your mind be free.

JACINTA HUDSON

Scrubbing here.
Rinsing there.
The problem with cleaning is it's everywhere.
Washing here.
Folding there.
The problem with housework, it's not going anywhere.
Sweeping here.
Mopping there.
It feels like an endless fight that doesn't seem fair.
Paper towel goes here.
Brush and shovel over there.
Pack away supplies now and breathe in fresh clean air.

WHEN STRAIGHT LINES AREN'T

☙❧

Procrastination is my jam.
You have to know this of me.
I have all the power in my hands,
But laziness, it owns me.
My to-do lists keep on growing.
And you don't have to show me.
The important tasks are glowing.
But a lack of effort slows me.
The longer that I wait,
I can feel the pressure mounting.
I'm running out of time.
As weeks, days, hours I am counting.

I want to look into your eyes deeply.
I want to see the world that lives in there.
I want to hold your body tightly.
And feel the warmth coming from your hair.
I want to play with you so sweetly,
Running laps from here to there.
I want the chance to love you intensely.
And provide for you the life that's more than fair.

WHEN STRAIGHT LINES AREN'T

∞

I love you.
I love you.
I love you, baby.
Yes, I do.
And I would do.
I would do.
Anything for you.
Coz, baby, I love you.

JACINTA HUDSON

You were the words inside my heart.
And you flowed through me so easy.
But then the words changed,
And so did my heart,
And now it isn't so breezy.

WHEN STRAIGHT LINES AREN'T

❧

I'm not gonna say it.
I'm not gonna be the one.
To jinx us all to hades.
And ruin all the fun.

Please don't be the one to say it.
Please don't mess this up.
Button it, zip it, and throw the key away.
For the love of god people, shut up!

You're everything I dreamed of, and then a little more.
Your aptitude for learning has my jaw hitting the floor.
You've got a spark of personality, and one that I adore.
The focus in your eyes is like you've been here once before.
Every crinkle in your frown and every giggle makes me sure.
I will spend my whole eternity making room for you to soar.

WHEN STRAIGHT LINES AREN'T

❧❦

You're the blessing I needed,
To keep my head afloat.
You're the rope ladder,
To help me get back on the boat.
You're the reason I kept on fighting,
When I felt that I would fall.
You're the reason I live my life,
You're my everything, my all.

JACINTA HUDSON

You call it freedom, but you're not free.
And it's this we plainly see.
You say you're strong, but you can't win.
You pay the price for others' sins.
You say you're learning, and you'll grow.
But how, I'm not convinced you know.
You say you're one, but that's a lie.
How many more will have to die?

WHEN STRAIGHT LINES AREN'T

Watching from a distance,
Wishing I could help you out.
But a little glad I am safe back here.
Watching from a distance,
As I hear you cry and shout.
And feeling incredibly lucky way down here.
Watching from a distance,
Wishing I could lend a hand.
But feeling oh so blessed from way back here.
Watching from a distance,
As you burn the promise land.
Sending you my love from way down here.

Nose to the grindstone.
It's time to get to work.
Cause I don't want the what-ifs anymore.

Nose to the grindstone.
It's time to get to work.
It's time to open up my wings, leap off the cliff and soar.

WHEN STRAIGHT LINES AREN'T

❦

They say it can't be done.
But I'm a stubborn one.
So, watch me as I start to climb this hill.
They think that it won't work.
But I'm not the type to shirk.
You think that I can't do it, but I will.

JACINTA HUDSON

You're sneaky and slimy.
You like to creep up on me.
You're sadistic, and blimey,
I never see you coming.
You catch me off guard.
Just when I think I'm free.
Getting past you is hard.
But I will keep on fighting.

WHEN STRAIGHT LINES AREN'T

❧

It's too loud and I can't hear.
It's too bright and I can't see.
It's too much and I can't feel.
All I want is to be free.
Free of the racing in my chest,
And the racing in my mind.
Free of the pounding of my heart.
Free of restrictions bound by time.
Because it's me against the world.
But the world is so much bigger.
I feel like I'm never catching up.
So, I'll never be the winner.

Balance is an illusion.
A fallacy.
A myth.
For true balance doesn't really exist.
Perfection is delusion.
Misconception.
Fairy-tale.
Strive all you like; it will be missed.

Hands up all the people with too much on their plate.
The ones who just keep adding, hoping it will fit.
Hands up all the people who have too many plates.
Pretending that they're fine and they won't tip.
Hands up all the people who juggle all their plates.
Hoping that they can catch them all.
Hands up all the people refusing help with all their plates.
Stubbornly watching them as they fall.

JACINTA HUDSON

Give me everything I want.
Not just everything I need.
Come on now, don't hold back.
Give me all the things now, please.

You give me everything I want,
Because you're everything I need.
And I don't have to hold back.
Now that it's you and me.

WHEN STRAIGHT LINES AREN'T

୨୧

Congratulations America.
This is your special day.
Moving from past transgressions.
Onto a better way.

Congrats to you America.
My hat goes off to you.
Now you must do the hard work.
From the old to something new.

Do you believe in second chances?
Do you believe we live again?
With a chance to mend old fences.
And reunite with friends.

Do you believe our souls survive death?
And through the years they roam.
Waiting for a child's first breath,
To return them safely home.

WHEN STRAIGHT LINES AREN'T

☙❧

As the list grows,
See me go,
Walking out the door.

Netflix can wait,
I've got a date,
With a great long list of chores.

There's a list of dreams,
As deep as the sea,
And it's calling out my name.

I've got things to do,
And so do you,
So, strap in and seize the day.

JACINTA HUDSON

❧

I have a little dream that I wish to see come true.
A collection sitting on my shelf.
Poetry written by myself.
About the life that we live through.

I have a little dream that I plan to pursue.
From happy to sad.
Excited to mad.
A series of emotions, red and blue.

I have a little dream, and I plan to share it with you.
A life full of nightmares and dreams.
And all of the emotional extremes.
A series of poetry with a fresh new do.

I have a little dream, and I can't wait to see it come true.
A collection of books.
All with matching looks.
And emotive titles too.

WHEN STRAIGHT LINES AREN'T

JACINTA HUDSON

ACKNOWLEDGMENTS

I want to say a big thank you to everyone who submitted title ideas for When Straight Lines Aren't. I know it sounds like a line, but I literally couldn't have gotten this book out in time without your help. I have professional-level skill in procrastinating and overthinking when attempting to title my books.

But the biggest thank you goes to Chelsea- aka, The Peachy Writer- for her initially odd, but ultimately brilliantly fitting, suggestion. Her title suggestion was a marvelous fit for a book whipped together in less than a year, reflecting the insanity of the current climate, and the strange way in which I- and many others- have utilized the current chaos to raise their voices and spur sudden progress in their passions and careers.
Even though her suggestion wasn't used in the end, it so perfectly incapsulated the essence of the book that I was able to use it to guide my search for a new title. It was her title suggestion that showed me the true meaning of the book.
Thank you.
x

ABOUT THE AUTHOR

Jacinta is the author of poetry books, Just a Thought and Emotional Ramblings. Residing in Victoria, Australia, she is a new mother, learning to juggle parenting with her love of writing. She has a blog, on her website, where she shares her experiences as a "newbie" writer and her advice to those who feel the same.

CONNECT WITH JACINTA

www.jacintahudson.com
www.instagram.com/jacintahudson
www.facebook.com/JacintaHudsonWriting

www.ingramcontent.com/pod-product-compliance
Lightning Source LLC
Chambersburg PA
CBHW070309010526
44107CB00056B/2540